Discover Deadly Animals

by Katrina Streza

© 2017 by Katrina Streza
ISBN: 978-1-53240-211-1
eISBN: 978-1-53240-212-8
Images licensed from Fotolia.com
All rights reserved.
No portion of this book may be reproduced
without express permission of the publisher.
First Edition
Published in the United States by
Xist Publishing
www.xistpublishing.com
PO Box 61593 Irvine, CA 92602

This is a male lion. Male lions roar to warn away other lions and animals. Lions kill other animals, or prey, with their sharp claws and teeth.

3

4

Most tigers hunt alone. These big cats come out at night to find, or stalk, their prey. Tigers are good swimmers. They can also dig holes to cover their food.

Mountain lions are quiet. They listen for their prey and sneak up behind it. Mountain lions kill small animals like mice and big animals like deer.

8

Brown bears use their long claws to catch fish, kill foxes, and dig up roots. Some brown bears like to eat human food and use their claws to break open trash bags.

Polar Bears hunt in the sea and on the snow. They like to eat seals, but they will eat anything--even humans.

11

A hippopotamus can hold her breath for five minutes. If she thinks anyone will hurt her baby, she will quickly attack. Some hippos kill crocodiles, lions, and people who come too close.

13

14

Wild boar eat plants, bugs, eggs, fish, and dead animals. They use their tusks to fight back against tigers, wolves, people and alligators.

The Egyptian cobra uses venom to kill his prey and keep his home safe. They like the shade and can sneak into houses. The Egyptian cobra lives in Africa.

17

Rattlesnakes live in the Americas and kill mice and small birds with venom. These snakes shake their tails to scare away other animals, but sometimes people get too close.

Alligators like to live alone. They use their big jaws and teeth to fight other animals. Alligators pull their prey under the water to eat.

A Killer Whale, or Orca, eats seals, squid, sea lions and dolphins. Their teeth grow to be ten centimeters long.

Piranhas live in rivers or lakes and have very strong jaws. They can bite through silver hooks and human hands! They like to eat small fish, snails, shrimp and plants.

Puffer Fish are only deadly to the animals who try to eat them. They swim slowly and puff up to scare away bigger animals and warn that they have a poison inside.

Black Widow spiders have a red mark on their tummy. This warns people, and bigger animals to stay away--they bite! These spiders kill and eat each other.

Black Scorpions hide in the ground and sting their prey. They hunt at night for bugs, mice, and lizards.

www.ingramcontent.com/pod-product-compliance
Lightning Source LLC
LaVergne TN
LVHW010021070426
835507LV00001B/29